PREHISTORIC!

BEFORE THE DINOSAURS

by
David West

A⁺
Smart Apple Media

Published by Smart Apple Media, an imprint of Black Rabbit Books
P.O. Box 3263, Mankato, Minnesota 56002
www.blackrabbitbooks.com

Produced by David West 🧍🧍 Children's Books
6 Princeton Court, 55 Felsham Road, London SW15 1AZ

Designed and illustrated by David West

Special thanks to Dr. Ron Blakey for the maps on page 4 & 5

Copyright © 2014 David West Children's Books

Library of Congress Cataloging-in-Publication Data

West, David, 1956- author.
 Before the dinosaurs / David West.
    pages cm. -- (Prehistoric!)
 Audience: Grade 4 to 6.
 Includes index.
 ISBN 978-1-62588-082-6 (library binding)
 ISBN 978-1-62588-109-0 (paperback)
 1. Paleontology--Paleozoic--Juvenile literature. 2. Animals, Fossil--Juvenile literature. I. Title.
 QE725.W44 2015
 560.172--dc23
                                    2013036616

Printed in China
CPSIA compliance information: DWCB14CP
010114

9 8 7 6 5 4 3 2 1

Contents

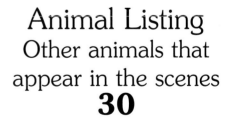

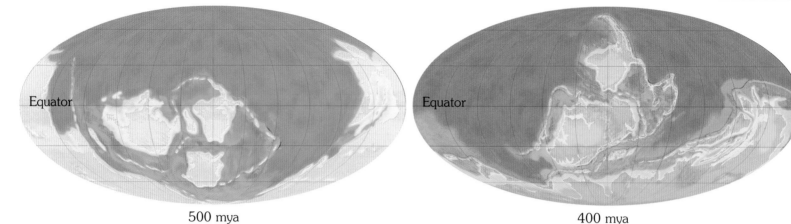

| 541 | | 490 | | 443 | 420 |
| CAMBRIAN | | | ORDOVICIAN | SILURIAN | |

Major diversification of life in this period with all animal forms living in the sea. **CO_2 is 35 times present-day levels.**

Invertebrates diversify into many new types. First green plants and fungi appear on land.

First jawed fish and armored jawless fish populate the seas.

The Paleozoic Era

The Paleozoic was a time of huge geological, climactic, and **evolutionary change**. It is subdivided into six geologic periods: the Cambrian, Ordovician, Silurian, Devonian, Carboniferous, and Permian. Life began in the ocean but eventually moved onto land. The Paleozoic Era ended with the largest **mass extinction** in the history of Earth, the Permian–Triassic extinction event. It took 30 million years for life to recover, paving the way for the age of the dinosaurs.

4

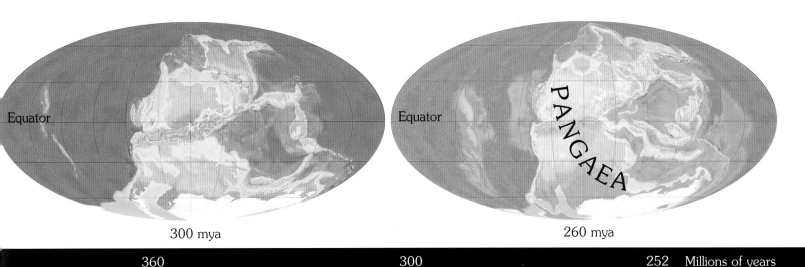

300 mya

260 mya

360		300		252 Millions of years ago (mya)
DEVONIAN		**CARBONIFEROUS**		**PERMIAN**
First clubmosses, horsetails, and ferns appear.		Amphibians common and diverse. First reptiles and coal forests. Highest-ever atmospheric oxygen levels.		Landmasses unite into supercontinent, Pangaea. Permian-Triassic extinction event occurs 252 mya: 95% of life on Earth becomes extinct.

THE PALEOZOIC EARTH
The Paleozoic started shortly after the breakup of a supercontinent called Pannotia. Throughout the early Paleozoic, Earth's landmass was broken up into a number of continents. Toward the end of the era, the continents gathered together into a supercontinent called Pangaea, which included most of Earth's land area.

Giant dragonflies, the size of eagles, inhabited the Carboniferous landscape.

5

1

3

Cambrian Ocean

Half a billion years ago, one of the strangest-looking hunters was discovered in the oceans of the Cambrian period. Named the *Anomalocaris*, it was the top predator of its time.

Anomalocaris had a large body, spiny grasping claws protruding from the front of its head, and teeth-like serrations around its mouth. Its eyes were set on stalks. Scientists have discovered that *Anomalocaris* had compound eyes like those of a fly. The eyes had 16,700 lenses,

Two *Anomalocarises* (1) hunt for **trilobites** (2). An *Opabinia* (3) searches for soft-bodied animals with its fanged **proboscis**. A *Marrella* (4) scavenges for food on the seabed while a strange worm-like creature called *Hallucigenia* (5) walks the edge of a sponge.

which gave it a huge advantage for locating prey. *Anomalocaris* preyed on trilobites that were 4 inches (10 cm) long. Scientists know this because broken remains appear in the **coprolites** of *Anomalocaris*. It swam by undulating the 11 pairs of overlapping flaps along its sides, catching the trilobites with its segmented limbs at the front.

Anomalocaris grew up to 3.3 feet (1 m) long.

7

Giant Sea Scorpions

The giant sea scorpion, *Pterygotus,* was one of the top predators in the sea and the largest sea scorpion to evolve. It lived in the shallow coastal waters around the world, hunting fish and trilobites.

Fossils of *Pterygotus* also have been found in habitats such as fresh water lakes many miles from the sea. Scientists think *Pterygotus* may have entered these lakes by chasing fish up rivers. The adults were far too big to travel over land. Younger, and therefore, smaller,

A *Pterygotus* (1) captures a trilobite (2) in coastal waters of the Devonian seas. Jawless fish called *Pteraspis* (3) and *Doryaspis* (4) swim close by. These armor-plated fish probably fed on **plankton**.

Pterygotuses may have been able to leave the water for short periods. It was a good swimmer, flapping its tail up and down to move swiftly through the water. It probably ambushed its prey by hiding in the sand, leaping out when a fish came close, and grabbing it with its claws. *Pterygotuses* were vulnerable to attack by larger predators such as *Dunkleosteus* (see pages 12–13).

Pterygotus grew up to 9.2 feet (2.8 m) long.

2

Lungs and Plates

One of the strangest fish to evolve out of the Devonian seas were the lungfish. These fish had gills and lungs, which allowed them to breathe in and out of water. *Scaumenacia* is one of the best known lungfish although it probably used its gills more than its lungs.

Scaumenacia had a crushing toothplate for feeding on hard-shelled prey. Stomach contents of fossils reveal a meal of *Asmusia*, a small **crustacean** protected by two shells. One *Scaumenacia* had swallowed

In a freshwater lake, three *Scaumenacias* (1) swim through the flooded forest looking for crustaceans. A group of armored fish called *Bothriolepis* (2) swim over a submerged trunk. On the mud below, a *Drepanaspis* (3) searches for food.

thousands of *Asmusia* before its death. The size of its back fin and **dorsal fin** suggest it had a powerful acceleration—probably to avoid predators. Fossils containing several fish suggest that they lived together in schools. Other freshwater fish during this period include **placoderms**. Plated fish such as *Bothriolepis* and *Drepanaspis* also lived in salt water. *Drepanaspis* had an unusual shape of a frying pan and was probably a bottom feeder like modern flounders.

Scaumenacia grew to 2.1 feet (64 cm) long.

1

2

Ocean Giant

One of the largest armored fish lived in the Devonian seas. Its name was *Dunkleosteus* and it was one of the top predators of its time.

Instead of teeth, *Dunkleosteus* had two pairs of sharp, bony plates that formed a beak-like structure. It could open its mouth very quickly, which created a powerful suction motion. This dragged any nearby fish into its mouth. Large prey would have been sliced in half by its incredibly strong bite.

A *Dunkleosteus* (1) rises out of the depths to snatch a primitive shark called *Stethacanthus* (2) with its bony plated teeth. Jellyfish (3) rise to the surface in this scene from the Upper Devonian seas.

As it was heavily armored, *Dunkleosteus* was a slow, but powerful, swimmer. It probably fed on other armored fish and early sharks such as *Stethacanthus*. This strange-looking shark had a flat top dorsal fin, which was covered in tiny tooth-shaped scales. Although it was small for a shark, it was a fast swimmer, feeding on fish and primitive squid.

Dunkleosteus grew up to 33 feet (10 m) long and weighed 4 tons (3.6 mt).

13

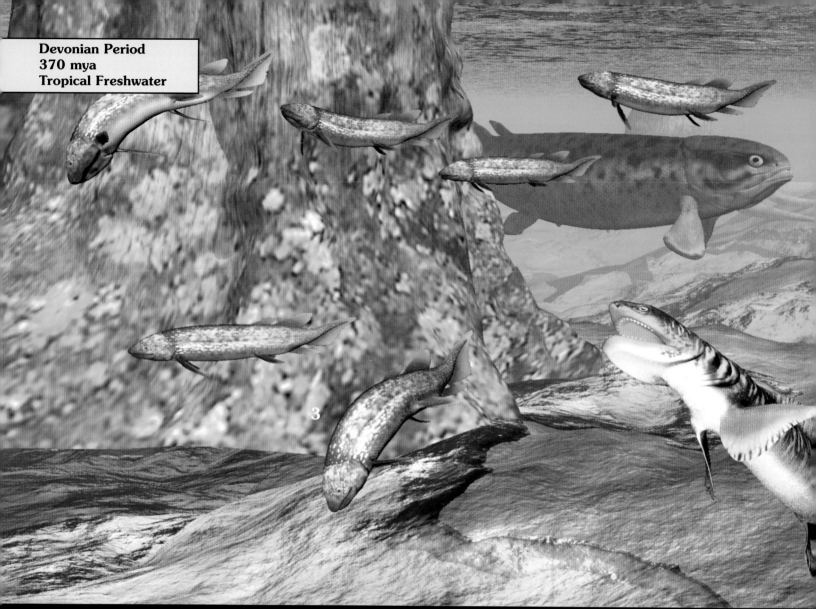

3

Freshwater Hunters

Rhizodus was a predatory **lobe-finned fish** with a mouth full of spiky teeth. It grew to huge sizes and holds the record for the largest freshwater fish ever to have lived.

Rhizodus had an extremely powerful bite. Darting out from a hiding place among roots or aquatic vegetation, it would capture its prey with its sharp teeth. Its prey probably included large sharks, lungfish, other lobe-finned fish, and even early amphibians such as *Hynerpeton*.

A *Rhizodus* (1) launches an attack on a pair of freshwater sharks called *Orthacanthus* (2). In turn, the sharks are hunting a school of lungfish called *Dipterus* (3) in a shallow river during the Upper Devonian period.

Freshwater sharks, such as *Orthacanthus*, hunted in the same lakes and rivers. It had a long spine growing from the back of its skull and a long dorsal fin that ran along its back, giving it the appearance of an eel. Its body reached nearly 10 feet (3 m) in length, and its mouth was crowded with a set of double-fanged teeth.

Rhizodus grew up to 23 feet (7 m) long.

15

Swamp Giants

During the Carboniferous period, high levels of oxygen led to an abundance of giant spiders, insects, and **arthropods**. The *Arthropleura*, with a segmented body and approximately 120 legs, looked like a centipede.

Arthropleura was the largest land arthropod ever. With its powerful set of sharp claws, it ate plants, small animals, and insects. It lived in the flooded swampy forests of this period. Scientists think it might have been able to travel underwater. It may have returned to the water

A giant centipede-looking creature called *Arthropleura* (1) rears up in defense against a large *Eogyrinus* (2). *Dendrerpetons* (3) flee for safety as giant dragonflies called *Meganeura* (4) search for small amphibians in this scene from the Carboniferous period.

each time it molted its shell. When molting it would have been vulnerable to attack by large fish and amphibians such as *Eogyrinus*. At 15-feet-long (4.6 m), the **tetrapod** was a giant predator that hunted like modern crocodiles. It would lie beneath the surface waiting for its prey to wander by. Smaller tetropods, such as *Dendrerpeton,* hunted smaller prey and, in turn, were prey to larger amphibians and fish.

Arthropleura was about 8.5 feet (2.6 m) long.

Shark Attack

The oceans of the late Carboniferous were home to one of the strangest-looking sharks, *Edestus*. The size of a great white shark, these monsters had a single set of upper and lower teeth that protruded from their mouth in a curve.

Scientists are unsure how it ate or what it fed on. As its teeth were serrated, it is likely that it was a meat eater. Like a pair of monstrous shears, its mouth would have sliced its prey in half before devouring it.

In the shallows of a Carboniferous sea, a large shark called *Edestus* (1) attacks an early marine reptile called *Mesosaurus* (2) as it chases after fish.

At about the same time, a marine reptile called *Mesosaurus* was swimming in the saltwater seas and estuaries. It was about 3.3 feet (1 m) in length with webbed feet, a slim body, and a long tail with a fin. Its long jaws had sharp teeth that were ideal for catching slippery fish. The nostrils at the end of its snout allowed it to breathe by poking them above the surface like modern crocodiles. *Mesosaurus* might have been able to move on land for short periods.

Edestus grew to about 20 feet (6.1 m) long.

1

Permian Pond

A variety of insectivorous amphibians, known as **lepospondyls**, lived in the rivers, lakes, and swamps of Permian North America. One of the strangest looking of these was *Diplocaulus*.

Diplocaulus was a newt-like, four-legged amphibian with a distinctive flattened and triangular-shaped head. Two bones at the back of its head had become elongated on each side to form a boomerang-shaped triangle. The body was short, ending in a finned tail. Its legs were quite

20

Diplocaulus (1), a group of newt-like animals, feed on aquatic crustaceans and plants. Dragonflies called *Meganeura* (2) move above the pond where horsetails grow in this scene from the middle Permian.

weak. Experts think it traveled through the water moving its body up and down, rather than using its tail like a fish. It may have lived in ponds and streams using its strange head as a form of water wing to steer like a submarine's **hydrofoil**. Alternatively, its head could have been shaped as it is to deter predators from trying to swallow it.

Diplocaulus grew up to 3.3 feet (1 m) long and weighed about 22 pounds (10 kg).

21

Dimetrodon

Due to the large sail on its back, *Dimetrodon* is one of the most recognizable animals that predate the dinosaurs. Scientists think it may have been used like the radiator in a car to help keep it cool or even to warm it up in the early morning sunshine. Others suggest it might have been used in courtship displays.

Dimetrodon was one of the top predators in the early Permian period. It fed on fish such as the freshwater shark, *Xenacanthus*, reptiles, and

A pair of *Dimetrodons* (1) approach two *Eryops* (2) who have taken refuge in a river. In the background male *Cotylorhynchuses* (3) create a rumpus in this scene from the early Permian period of what is today North America.

amphibians such as *Diplocaulus* and *Eryops*. Although *Eryops* was a large predator, it was no match for the more powerful *Dimetrodon*. The larger *Cotylorhynchus*, which measured up to 20 feet (6.1 m) and weighed as much as 2 tons (1.8 metric tons), was too big to fear any predators.

Dimetrodon was around 10 feet (3 m) in length and weighed up to 550 pounds (249 kg).

Permian Period
260 mya
South Africa

Head Butting

At 1 ton (0.9 mt), *Moschops* was the largest land animal in its environment. Heavily built, it had the splayed out legs typical of a reptile. Its teeth were sharp and suited to cutting vegetation. It had a very large gut for digesting tough plant matter.

Moschops probably lived in small herds as scientists have discovered several individuals fossilized together. *Moschops* had a thick skull, which was 4 inches (10 cm) thick in places. Scientists think it may

A group of *Keratocephaluses* (1) move away from the lush vegetation of a swampy lake as a herd of *Moschops* (2) move in during the middle Permian period of what is today South Africa.

have head-butted rivals during the mating season similar to modern-day rams. Another thick-headed **dinocephalian** living in South Africa was *Keratocephalus*, which means "horned head." It had a large, bony area protruding from its head. Smaller than *Moschops*, it grew to 9.8 feet (3 m) long.

Moschops was about 16 feet (4.9 m) long and weighed about 1 ton (0.9 mt).

Permian Russia

Mammal-like hunters appeared during the Permian period. The largest of these was *Inostrancevia*, a giant **gorgonopsid**. Like a saber-toothed tiger, it had large, canine teeth that were 5.9 inches (15 cm) long.

Inostrancevia had a long, slender body, short legs, a short tail, and a massive head that was 24 inches (61 cm) long. It was the top predator in its environment and hunted **pareiasaurs** such as *Scutosaurus* and maybe even the large **omnivorous therapsid**, *Estemmenosuchus*.

This scene is from the Middle Permian period in what is now Russia. A pair of *Inostrancevia* (1) chase off a couple of young *Doliosauriscuses* (2) on a stony beach by a river. A large *Estemmenosuchus* (3) is in the foreground.

Other predators might have been on the menu, such as *Doliosauriscus*. This dinocephalian was a large carnivore that grew up to 13 feet (4 m). Other dinocephalians, such as *Estemmenosuchus*, grew even larger and up to 16.5 feet (5 m). These omnivores had large horn-like structures growing from their heads, which were probably used as courtship displays.

Inostrancevia grew up to 11.5 feet (3.5 m) long and weighed about 1,000 pounds (454 kg).

Wolf-like Hunters

Like the modern-day wolves from which it takes its name, *Lycaenops* may have hunted in packs. It had a long, slender skull with a set of dog-like fangs that were ideal for stabbing and tearing at the flesh of any large prey.

Lycaenops moved with its long legs held close to its body like modern day mammals. This was unusual as most animals at this time moved with their legs to the sides of their bodies. The ability to move like a

A pack of *Lycaenops* (1) chase down a pair of **dicynodonts** called *Lystrosaurus* (2). In the background, a herd of large dinocephalians called *Titanosuchus* (3) feed on plants in this scene from the late Permian Period in what we know as South Africa.

mammal gave *Lycaenops* an advantage over its prey as it could outrun them. Its body might also have been covered in fur. *Lycaenops* probably hunted small reptiles and dicynodonts such as *Lystrosaurus*. These slower moving animals were heavily built plant eaters and approximately the size of a pig. Their sharp beaks and tusks were no match for a hungry pack of *Lycaenops*.

Lycaenops grew up to 3.3 feet (1 m) long and weighed 33 pounds (15 kg).

Animal Listing

Other animals that appear in the scenes.

Bothriolepis
(pp. 10–11)
Placoderm
12 inches (30 cm)
long
Oceans

Cotylorhynchus
(pp. 22–23)
Caseidid
20 feet (6.1 m) long
North America

Dendrerpeton
(pp. 16–17)
Temnospondyl
3.3 feet (1 m) long
North America,
Europe

Dipterus
(pp. 14–15)
Theropod dinosaur
14 inches (36 cm)
long
Tropical freshwater

Doliosauriscus
(pp. 26–27)
Dinocephalian
13 feet (4 m) long
Russia

Doryaspis
(pp. 8–9)
Primitive jawless fish
6 inches (15 cm)
long
Oceans

Drepanaspis
(pp. 10–11)
Primitive jawless fish
12 inches (30 cm)
long
Ocean

Eogyrinus
(pp. 16–17)
Anthracosaurid
15 feet (4.6 m) long
Europe

Eryops
(pp. 22–23)
Temnospondyl
5 feet (1.5 m) long
North America

Estemmenosuchus
(pp. 26–27)
Dinocephalian
16.5 feet (5 m) long
Russia

Hallucigenia
(pp. 6–7)
Unknown
1.3 inches (3 cm)
long
Ocean

Keratocephalus
(pp. 24–25)
Dinocephalian
9.8 feet (3 m) long
South Africa

Lystrosaurus
(pp. 28–29)
Dicynodont
3 feet (0.9 m) long
Antarctica, India,
and South Africa

Marrella
(pp. 6–7)
Arthropod
0.8 inches (2 cm)
long
Ocean

Meganeura
(pp. 16–17, 20–21)
Insect
25.6 inches (65 cm)
wingspan
Europe

Mesosaurus
(pp. 18–19)
Reptile
12 inches (30 cm)
long
Southern Africa and
South America

Opabinia
(pp. 6–7)
Arthropod
3 inches (7.6 cm)
long
Ocean

Orthacanthus
(pp. 14–15)
Freshwater shark
10 feet (3 m) long
Europe and North
America.

Pteraspis
(pp. 8–9)
Jawless fish
7.8 inches (20 cm)
long
Ocean

Stethacanthus
(pp. 12–13)
Shark
5 feet (1.5 m) long
Ocean

Titanosuchus
(pp. 28–29)
Dinocephalian
8.2 feet (2.5 m) long
South Africa

Glossary

anthracosaurid A member of a group of usually large aquatic Amphibians from the Carboniferous and Permian periods.

arthropod An animal which has a segmented body, jointed limbs, and usually a shell that includes insects, spiders, scorpions, and crustaceans.

caseidid A member of an extinct group of very primitive plant-eating, mammal-like reptiles.

CO_2 Carbon dioxide.

coprolites The fossilized remains of an animal's poo.

crustacean Water-living arthropod with a hard shell, including lobsters, shrimps, crabs, and barnacles.

dicynodonts An extinct group of mammal-like reptiles with two tusks.

dinocephalian A member of an extinct group of large-bodied, early therapsids that lived during the Permian period.

dorsal fin A fin located on the back of a fish or sea mammal.

evolutionary change To change by natural selection over a long period of time.

fossils The remains of living things that have turned to rock.

gorgonopsid A member of an extinct group of meat-eating therapsids.

hydrofoil A structure that works like an underwater wing, designed to lift the hull of a boat or submarine when it is moving.

lepospondyl A member of an extinct group of small amphibians.

lobe-finned fish Bony fish with fleshy, lobed, paired fins, which are joined to the body by a single bone.

mass extinction A large-scale disappearance of species of animals and plants in a relatively short period of time.

omnivorous Eating both animals and plants.

pareiasaur A member of the family of extinct, large, plant-eating reptiles that flourished during the Permian period.

placoderm An extinct class of armored prehistoric fish, which lived from the late Silurian to the end of the Devonian period.

plankton Minute organisms that live in water and are incapable of swimming against a current. They are a valuable food source to many marine animals.

proboscis An elongated tube from the head, used for feeding.

temnospondyl A type of large, extinct, primitive amphibian.

tetrapod A member of the large family of animals that includes the first four-limbed vertebrates and their descendants, and the living and extinct amphibians, reptiles, birds, and mammals.

therapsid An extinct group of mammal-like reptiles.

trilobite An extinct, sea-living arthropod which was oval in shape.

Index